PUSH or PULL

Susan Canizares
Betsey Chessen

Scholastic Inc.
New York • Toronto • London • Auckland • Sydney

Acknowledgments

Literacy Specialist: Linda Cornwell

National Science Consultant : David Larwa

Design: Bryce Schimanski

Photo Research: Amla Sanghvi

Endnotes: Mary Hart

Endnote Illustrations: Craig Spearing

Photographs: Cover: Dugald Bremner/ Tony Stone Images; pg. 1: Elyse Lewin/ Image Bank; pg. 2: Myrleen Ferguson Cate/Photo Edit; pg. 3: Paul Barton/Stock Market; pg. 4: Stan Godlewski/Tony Stone Images; pg. 5: Bob Torrez/Tony Stone Images; pg. 6: Stephen Frisch/Stock Boston; pg. 7: T & D McCarthy/Stock Market; pg.8: Bob Daemmrich/Stock Boston; pg. 9: Telegraph Colour Library/FPG; pg. 10: Dugald Bremner/ Tony Stone Images; pg. 11: C. J. Allen/Stock Boston; pg. 12: Bill Losh/FPG

Library of Congress Cataloging-in-Publication Data
Canizares, Susan 1960-
Push and pull/Susan Canizares, Betsey Chessen.
p.cm. --(Science emergent readers)
Summary: Simple text and photographs explore the many things that can
be moved by pushing or pulling, from swings and mowers to wagons and ropes.
ISBN 0-439-08119-X (pbk.: alk. paper)
1. Mechanics--Juvenile literature. 2. Force and energy--Juvenile literature.
[1. Force and energy. 2. Mechanics] I. Chessen, Betsey, 1970-. II. Title. III. Series.
QC127.4.C36 1999

531--dc21

98-53316
CIP AC

3   4   5   6   7   8   9   10   08   03   02   01   00   99

Push and pull.

Push a swing.

Push a lawn mower.

Pull a wagon.

Pull a bow.

Push a stroller.

Push a button.

Pull a rope.

Pull a ball.

Push

and pull.

Push or pull?

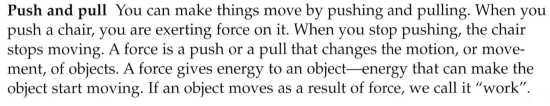

PUSH or PULL

Push and pull You can make things move by pushing and pulling. When you push a chair, you are exerting force on it. When you stop pushing, the chair stops moving. A force is a push or a pull that changes the motion, or movement, of objects. A force gives energy to an object—energy that can make the object start moving. If an object moves as a result of force, we call it "work".

Push a swing When you pull the swing back and release it, the number of back and forth movements will be the same whether or not a person is sitting in the swing. The weight of the person makes no difference in how many times the swing goes forward and backward. The number of back and forth movements of the swing depends on the height of the swing and the strength of the force that pushes it.

Push a lawn mower When you push a lawn mower, the wheels turn and the mower goes forward. The forward motion makes the blades go round and round. This is an easy way to cut the grass.

Pull a wagon When you pull a heavy load, you pull with your muscles. A load pulled on a bumpy road will feel heavier than the same load pulled on a smooth road, and your muscles will have to work harder. A wagon pulled on a rough road is slowed down by bumps. A smooth road has very small bumps, so the wagon can roll easily.

Pull a bow Gravity is the force that pulls every object toward the ground. It is the force of gravity that makes an object fall from the sky to the earth. It is because of gravity that an arrow won't sail through the air forever but will eventually fall to the ground.

Push a stroller It is easy and quick to move things on wheels. The simple wheel is one of the most important machines ever invented. Wheels are made of all sorts of materials, such as wood, plastic, metal, and rubber. With wheels it is almost no work at all to move a stroller down the street.

Push a button You may not think of pushing a button as using your force, but every time you push a button on a telephone, doorbell, or elevator, that is exactly what you are doing. At the touch of a button, you can connect to the Internet and explore the World Wide Web, exchange e-mail messages with your friends, and do your homework.

Pull a rope During the game of tug-of-war, one team tries the pull the other team across a line to score points. The team that pulls the hardest wins. Tension in the tug-of-war rope transmits the force from one team to the other.

Pull a ball When something is pulled or pushed, it does not always move. Sometimes it changes shape instead. You can mold clay into any shape you want, and it will keep the new shape. Squeeze a ball, however, and it jumps back to its original shape as soon as you stop squeezing. Things that bounce back are elastic.

Push You can use your force to push a merry-go-round. You can then jump aboard, and the force you created will keep the merry-go-round spinning long after you have stopped pushing. Long enough to have a fun ride!

Pull Did you know that when you shuck corn you are using the force of pulling? You also use pushing and pulling when you peel vegetables, slice fruit, and drink through a straw. Each thing moves in its own way, so sometimes pushing and pulling can feel different, depending on what you are doing.

Push or pull? If two people who are about the same height and weight push and pull a wagon at the same time, the wagon won't move forward or backward. It stays in place because the people pushing and pulling are using the same amount of force at the same time. Since they are pushing and pulling against each other, in opposite directions, their movements cancel each other out.